ALTERNATIVE ROCK SHEET MUSIC

CONTENTS

CHASING CARS

Words and Music by GARY LIGHTBODY,
TOM SIMPSON, PAUL WILSON,
JONATHAN QUINN and NATHAN CONNOLLY

ZOMBIE

Lyrics and Music by
DOLORES O'RIORDAN

CRAZY

Words and Music by BRIAN BURTON,
THOMAS CALLAWAY, GIANPIERO REVERBERI
and GIANFRANCO REVERBERI

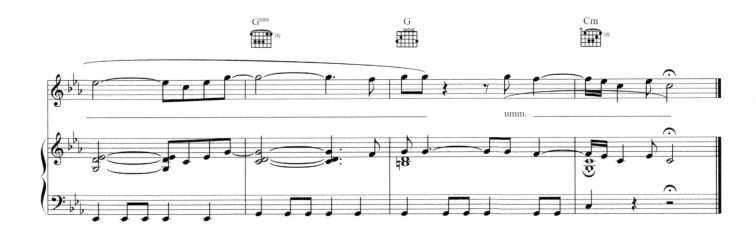

umm.

KARMA POLICE

Words and Music by THOMAS YORKE,
JONATHAN GREENWOOD, COLIN GREENWOOD,
EDWARD O'BRIEN and PHILIP SELWAY

GOOD RIDDANCE

(TIME OF YOUR LIFE)

Words by BILLIE JOE
Music by GREEN DAY

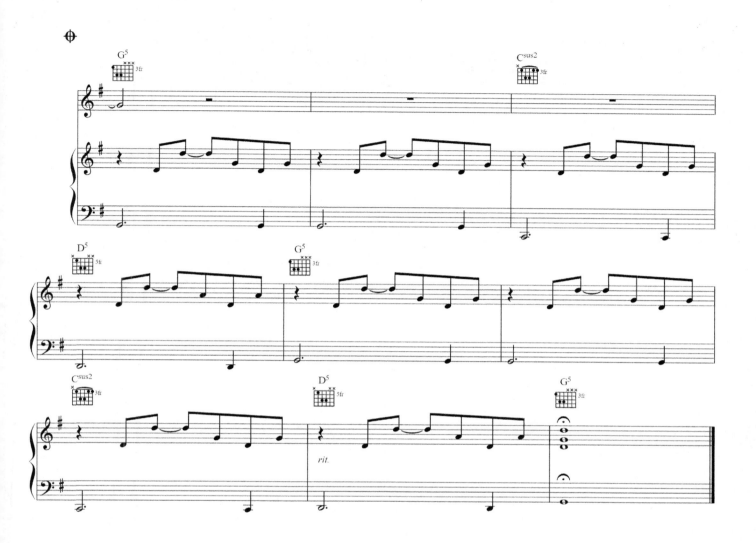

SEVEN NATION ARMY

Words and Music by
JACK WHITE

time   right   be - hind   my ___   back.
Eng - land   to   the   hounds   of ___   hell. ___
drip   out   of   ev - 'ry ___   pore. ___

And I'm   talk - ing   to   my - self   at ___   night ___
And   if   I   catch   it   com - ing   back   my ___   way, ___
And I'm   bleed - ing   and   I'm   bleed - ing   and   I'm

___   be - cause   I   can't   for - get. ___
___   I'm   gon - na   serve   it   to   you.
___   bleed - ing   right   be - fore   the ___   lord. ___

Back   and   forth   through   my ___   mind,
And   that   ain't   what   you   want   to   hear, ___
All   the   words   are   gon - na   bleed   from ___   me,

___   be - hind   a   cig - ar - ette. ___
___   but   that's ___   what   I'll ___   do. ___
___   and   I   will   think   no ___   more. ___

And the   mes - sage   com - ing   from   my   eyes ___
And the   feel - ing   com - ing   from   my   bones ___
And the   stains ___   com - ing   from   my   blood ___

G

f

says   leave it a - lone.
says   find   a home.
tell   me go back home.

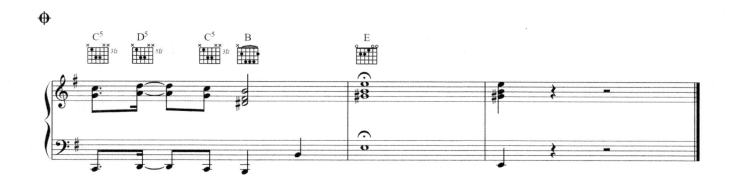

LOSING MY RELIGION

Words and Music by BILL BERRY,
PETER BUCK, MIKE MILLS
and MICHAEL STIPE

UPRISING

Words and Music by
MATTHEW BELLAMY

us.   We   will   be   vic -

-to - ri - ous.   So   come   on!

Hey!

Hey!

Hey!

Hey!

D.S. al Coda

WONDERWALL

Words and Music by
NOEL GALLAGHER

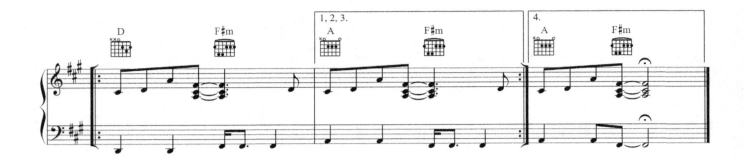

BLACK HOLE SUN

Words and Music by
CHRIS CORNELL

Won't you come? _____ Won't you come? .

Play 6 times

Hang my head,   drown my fear,   'til you   all   just dis-ap- pear. _____   Black hole

D.S. al Coda

Won't you come? _____

Won't you come? _____

LEARN TO FLY

Words and Music by TAYLOR HAWKINS,
NATE MENDEL and DAVE GROHL

Run and tell all of the an - gels this could take all night.
Think I'm dy - in' nurs - in' pa - tience. It can wait one night.

look - in' for some -thin' to help ___ me burn ___ out bright. _____

I'm look -in' for a com - pli - ca - tion, look -in' 'cause I'm tired of ly -
try -
try -

-in'. Make my way ___ back home ___ when I learn to fly high.
-in'. to fly
-in'. to...

high.

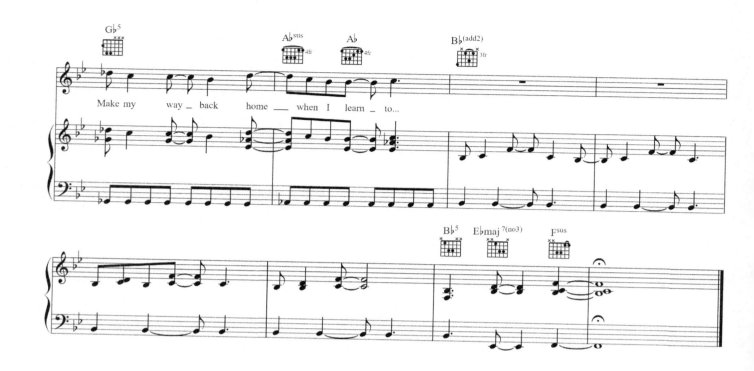

Make my way _ back home _ when I learn _ to...

IN THE END

Words and Music by ROB BOURDON,
BRAD DELSON, JOE HAHN,
MIKE SHINODA and CHARLES BENNINGTON

though I tried, ___ it all fell a-part. What it meant to me will e-ven-tual-ly be a mem-o-

though I tried, ___ it all fell a-part.

-ry of a time when I tried so hard. I tried so hard ___ and got so ___ far, ___

but in the end, ___ it does-n't e-ven mat-ter. I had to

D.S. al Coda

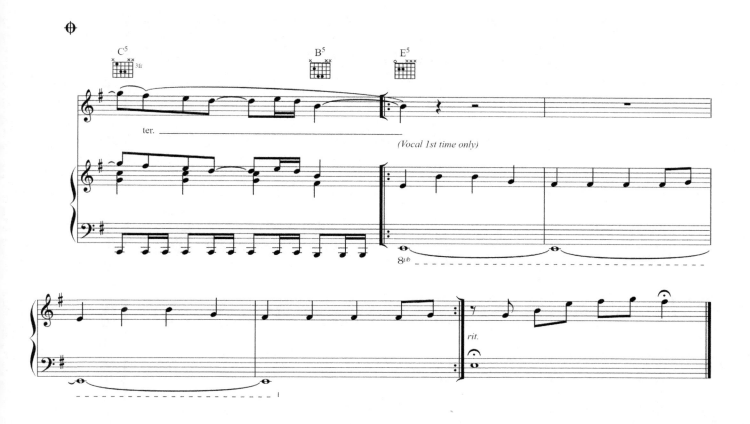

ter.

(Vocal 1st time only)

SMELLS LIKE TEEN SPIRIT

Words and Music by KURT COBAIN,
KRIST NOVOSELIC and DAVE GROHL

To Coda ⊕

RADIOACTIVE

Words and Music by DANIEL REYNOLDS,
BENJAMIN McKEE, DANIEL SERMON,
ALEXANDER GRANT and JOSH MOSSER

sun has - n't___ died.___ Deep in my___ bones,_

straight from in - side...___

D.S. al Coda

...I'm wak - ing

ra - di - o - ac - tive.

WHERE IS MY MIND?

Words and Music by
FRANK BLACK

I WILL FOLLOW YOU INTO THE DARK

Words and Music by
BENJAMIN GIBBARD

Then I'll fol - low you ____ in - to the dark.

slight rit.

SAY IT AIN'T SO

Words and Music by
RIVERS CUOMO

D.S. al Coda

91

You've cleaned up, found Je - sus, things are good or so I hear. This bot - tle of Stev - en's

a - wak - ens an - cient feel - ings. Like fa - ther, step - fa - ther, the son is drown - ing in the

flood, _____ yeah, yeah, yeah, __ yeah, yeah. __

Guitar solo

THNKS FR TH MMRS

Words and Music by PATRICK STUMP,
PETER WENTZ, ANDREW HURLEY and JOSEPH TROHMAN

thanks for the mem - o - ries. __ Thanks for the mem - o - ries. __ See, he tastes

like you, __ on - ly sweet - er, __ oh. __

WITH ARMS WIDE OPEN

Words and Music by SCOTT A. STAPP
and MARK T. TREMONTI

With arms wide

o - pen,

wide o - pen.

PLUSH

Words and Music by ERIC KRETZ,
ROBERT DeLEO, DEAN DeLEO
and SCOTT WEILAND

And I feel _____ that time's a wast-ed go. _____ So where you go-ing 'til to-
And I feel _____ so much de-pends _____ on the weath-er. So is it rain-ing in your

IRIS

FROM THE MOTION PICTURE CITY OF ANGELS

Words and Music by
JOHN RZEZNIK

And I'd give up for - ev - er to touch __ you 'cause I __ know __
I could taste __ is this mo - ment, and __ all __
fight the tears __ that ain't com - ing, or the __ mo -

__ that you feel __ me some - how. You're the clos - est to heav - en that I'll __
__ I can breath __ is your __ life. And soon - er or lat - er it's o -
- ment of truth __ in your __ lies. When ev - 'ry - thing feels like the mov-

When ev - 'ry - thing's _ made to be _ bro - ken

I just _ want _ you to know _ who I _ am.

UNDER THE BRIDGE

Words and Music by ANTHONY KIEDIS,
FLEA, JOHN FRUSCIANTE
and CHAD SMITH

Some-times I feel ___ like I don't have a part-ner.
drive on her streets ___ 'cause she's my com-pan-ion. I
hard to be-lieve ___ that there's no-bod-y out ___ there It's